THE GREAT WRIT

A Nation's Struggle

with Liberty and Power

Kerry Khan

Copyright © 2025 by Kerry Khan

All rights reserved. No part of this publication may be reproduced, distributed, or transmitted in any form or by any means, including photocopying, recording, or other electronic or mechanical methods, without the prior written permission of the author, except in the case of brief quotations embodied in critical reviews and certain other noncommercial uses permitted by copyright law.

Published by Record Press, The

www.krecordpress.com

ISBN: 979-8-9934480-1-5 (Paperback)

ISBN: 979-8-9934480-0-8 (E-book)

CONTENTS

Acknowledgments — iv

Introduction — 1

Chapter 1 — 4
The Foundational Tension

Chapter 2 — 7
The Great Writ in Crisis:
Lincoln and the Civil War

Chapter 3 — 13
Habeas in a World at War:
National Security and the Rights of Citizens

Chapter 4 — 20
The "War on Terror":
Guantanamo Bay and the
Redefinition of the Writ

Chapter 5: The Unfinished Argument — 27

Glossary — 31

Bibliography — 34

Acknowledgements

While the writing of a book is a solitary endeavor, its completion is never accomplished alone. This work would not have been possible without the support of a remarkable fellowship of family, friends, and colleagues.

My deepest gratitude is for my family, who weathered this long journey with unwavering patience and grace. To Myra, Lee, Munch, and Lee Jr.—your belief in this project was the steady foundation upon which it was built. You provided the sanctuary and encouragement necessary to confront the complex questions within these pages, and for that, I am eternally grateful.

I am also profoundly grateful to the friends and colleagues who engaged with these ideas in their nascent stages. Their rigorous feedback and challenging questions during late-night debates were instrumental in refining the central arguments of this book and saving me from many an error.

This book is a testament to a collective effort, and I am honored to have had such a formidable group of people at my side.

DEDICATION

To Myra, Lee, Munch, and Lee Jr. Your unwavering faith gave me the freedom to forge this tribute. It stands in sacred memory of the countless souls who sought this protection, and as a ready shield for all who need it every day.

The struggle endures.

Introduction

In October of 1864, an Indiana lawyer named Lambdin P. Milligan was arrested in his home by the U.S. Army. Accused of conspiracy and treason, he was tried not by a jury of his peers, but by a military commission, which sentenced him to be hanged. To the government, it was a necessary act of war to quell insurrection behind Union lines. To Milligan, it was an unconstitutional outrage. His only hope lay in a dusty, centuries-old legal tool—the writ of habeas corpus. The question at the heart of his case was simple and profound: in a time of crisis, does the Constitution yield to the power of the state, or does the state remain subject to the Constitution?

This question is the central theme of this book. The writ of habeas corpus, at its core, empowers individuals to ask, "Why am I being held?"—a question that has sparked some of the most significant constitutional battles in U.S. history. Its power lies in four key functions. First, it **forces justification**, compelling the executive to present a lawful reason for detention. Second, it **triggers independent judicial review**, empowering a judge to assess that reason. Third, it **operates on the individual level**, allowing any single person to challenge the full might of the state. Finally, it **creates a public record**, ensuring both legal and political accountability.

The central thesis of this work is that the writ exists in a state of permanent, dynamic tension. This is not a conflict between right and wrong, but between two competing constitutional goods: the judiciary's role as the guardian of individual rights and the political branches' (the President and Congress) responsibility to ensure national security. From the earliest days of the republic, this tension has shaped the writ's evolution, expanding and contracting its power in response to the pressures of rebellion, war, and fear.

To trace this evolution, this book follows a chronological path through the writ's greatest tests.

Chapter 1 establishes the foundational conflict by examining the writ's English origins and its opposing interpretations in the landmark cases of *Ex parte Bollman*[1] and *Ex parte McCardle*.[2] **Chapter 2** explores the writ's near-collapse during the Civil War under President Lincoln. **Chapter 3** analyzes its role during World War II. **Chapter 4** delves into its modern redefinition in the age of the War on Terror. Finally, **Chapter 5** synthesizes this history to assess the current state of the great writ today. Grasping the forces that have shaped habeas corpus is essential to understanding the character of the American nation—a continuous and vital argument about what it means to be both safe and free.

Notes

1. *Ex parte Bollman*, 8 U.S. 75 (1807).
2. *Ex parte McCardle*, 74 U.S. 506 (1869).

Chapter 1: The Foundational Tension

The writ of habeas corpus stands as "the great constitutional privilege,"[1] a foundational tool designed to safeguard individual liberty. At its core, this ancient legal instrument, whose Latin name means "you shall have the body," functions as a court order demanding that a public official deliver an imprisoned person to the court and provide a valid reason for their detention. Its roots stretch deep into English common law, with principles echoed in the Magna Carta of 1215, which first declared that no free man could be imprisoned "except by the lawful judgment of his equals or by the law of the land."[2] The writ evolved over centuries as a practical tool for the English courts to check the power of the Crown. It also served as a tool for strengthening the judiciary, the process by which central courts expanded their power and created a unified legal system. For centuries, the Court of King's Bench used the writ to assert its dominance over rival courts, creating the very precedent of a powerful, independent judiciary that the American founders would later embrace.[3]

This principle, however, contains a deep and persistent tension. In its most assertive form, exemplified by the powerful opinion of Chief Justice John Marshall in *Ex parte Bollman*, the writ is a profound instrument of judicial authority, enabling the courts to question and command the highest levels of the executive branch.[4] Yet, this power is not absolute. As the Supreme Court itself would later concede in *Ex parte McCardle*, the legislature holds a potent and decisive check. Congress holds the power to strip the judiciary of its **jurisdiction**—its authority to hear cases—over the writ, leaving the "great privilege" exposed to the political will of the moment.[5] This inherent conflict—between the writ as a sacred right and as a politically contingent tool—forms the central inquiry of this book.

Chapter 1 Summary:

- The writ of habeas corpus is an ancient legal tool, originating in English common law, that allows a person to challenge their detention.
- It was embraced by the American founders as a fundamental check on government power.

- A core tension exists in the U.S. Constitution: the judiciary acts as the writ's guardian (*Ex parte Bollman*), but Congress has the power to limit the courts' authority to hear habeas cases (*Ex parte McCardle*).

Notes

1. *Ex parte Bollman*, 8 U.S. 75, 95 (1807).
2. Magna Carta, cl. 39.
3. Paul D. Halliday, *Habeas Corpus: From England to Empire* (Cambridge, MA: Belknap Press, 2010), 15–20.
4. *Bollman*, 8 U.S. at 125.
5. *Ex parte McCardle*, 74 U.S. 506, 514 (1869).

Chapter 2: The Great Writ in Crisis: Lincoln and the Civil War

2.1 : The Crucible of War

The American Civil War was more than a military conflict; it was a constitutional crucible. Unlike any foreign war, this internal rebellion tore at the very fabric of the nation's laws, blurring the lines between battlefield and home front, citizen, and combatant. The existential threat was not just to the Union's borders, but to its survival as a constitutional republic. The established mechanics of justice, designed for a nation at peace, seemed utterly insufficient to confront a widespread insurrection that held popular support in nearly half the country.

At the center of this crisis stood President Abraham Lincoln, who faced a dilemma of unprecedented scale. He was bound by his oath to "preserve, protect, and defend the Constitution," yet the very act of preservation seemed to require actions that the Constitution constrained. The document's guarantee of the writ of habeas corpus, as detailed in the Suspension Clause,[1] stood as a potential obstacle to his ability to swiftly contain the rebellion. Lincoln was forced to grapple with a formidable question: could a president, in order to save the whole of the Constitution, temporarily disregard one of its most sacred parts? This was not just a legal problem; it was the central crisis of the executive branch, and its resolution would shape the limits of presidential power for all time.

2.2 : The Doctrine of Necessity

In response to this crisis, President Lincoln chose a course of unprecedented executive action. Citing his constitutional duty to "preserve, protect, and defend" the nation, he unilaterally suspended the writ of habeas corpus in certain regions without prior congressional approval. His justification, which he later articulated to Congress, was not rooted in a claim of absolute power, but in a doctrine of absolute necessity. He argued that the rebellion created a situation where the survival of the government itself was at stake. Faced with this reality, he posed a stark, pragmatic question that would echo through American history: "...are all the laws, *but one*, to go unexecuted, and the government itself go to pieces, lest that one be violated?"[2] For Lincoln, the answer was clear. He maintained that to save the constitutional order as a whole, the temporary and geographically limited suspension of one of its procedures was a necessary, if regrettable, act.

2.3 : The Supremacy of the Constitution

Years after the Civil War ended, with the Union preserved, the Supreme Court finally issued its powerful judicial response to the question of wartime executive power. In the landmark case of *Ex parte Milligan*, the Court addressed the fate of a civilian who had been sentenced to death by a military tribunal in Indiana—a state whose civil courts, crucially, had never ceased functioning during the war.[3] The Court's ruling was a forceful and unambiguous rebuke of the administration's actions.

Writing for the majority, Justice David Davis declared that the President had no constitutional authority to subject civilians to military justice when the civil courts were operational.

The "doctrine of necessity," the Court argued, could not be used to justify the suspension of fundamental constitutional rights. In one of the most famous passages in Supreme Court history, the Court laid down an enduring principle: "The Constitution of the United States is a law for rulers and people, equally in war and in peace, and covers with the shield of its protection all classes of men, at all times and under all circumstances."[4] The Milligan ruling, therefore, stands as the judiciary's ultimate answer to Lincoln's dilemma, asserting that the constitutional order is not a peacetime luxury, but an all-weather shield for liberty.

2.4 : The Historian's Verdict

The stark contrast between Lincoln's executive argument and the Court's judicial decree is complicated by historical reality. As historians like Mark E. Neely Jr. have shown, the actual use of the habeas suspension was often a messy, practical response to the chaos of war, rather than a grand constitutional philosophy in action.[5] The majority of arrests were not aimed at political dissenters but at disrupting the Confederate war effort in the volatile border states—an administrative and military necessity that the civil court

system was ill-equipped to handle.

This context suggests that both Lincoln's high-flown "doctrine of necessity" and the *Milligan* court's absolute "rule of law" doctrine may be too simplistic. Lincoln's actions, viewed through the lens of the on-the-ground reality, appear less like a tyrannical overreach and more like a pragmatic, if constitutionally questionable, response to a genuine crisis. At the same time, the *Milligan* ruling, while perhaps idealistic about the capabilities of civil courts during the war, was a critically **necessary** corrective. It served to firmly re-establish the supremacy of civil law after the crisis had passed, ensuring that the emergency measures of the war did not become a permanent feature of the American legal landscape. The great writ, therefore, was both bent by the necessity of the moment and ultimately reaffirmed by the enduring principles of the Constitution.

Chapter 2 Summary:

- The Civil War created a constitutional crisis, forcing President Lincoln to choose between upholding the writ

of habeas corpus and preserving the Union.
- Lincoln argued for a "doctrine of necessity," claiming his duty to save the nation allowed him to unilaterally suspend the writ.
- After the war, the Supreme Court in *Ex parte Milligan* powerfully rejected this, stating the Constitution applies equally in war and peace.
- The historical reality is nuanced, showing Lincoln's actions were a practical response to chaos, but the Court's ruling was a necessary corrective to re-establish the rule of law.

Notes

1. U.S. Const. art. I, § 9, cl. 2.
2. Abraham Lincoln, "Message to Congress in Special Session," July 4, 1861.
3. *Ex parte Milligan*, 71 U.S. 2 (1866).
4. *Milligan*, 71 U.S. at 120–21.
5. Mark E. Neely Jr., *The Fate of Liberty: Abraham Lincoln and Civil Liberties* (New York: Oxford University Press, 1991), 233–35.

Chapter 3: Habeas in a World at War: National Security and the Rights of Citizens

3.1 : A Nation at War, A People Apart

The United States' entry into World War II began with the shocking and traumatic attack on Pearl Harbor in December 1941. The event plunged the nation into a state of profound fear and a thirst for decisive action. On the West Coast, this war hysteria merged with a decades-long history of anti-Asian racism, creating a toxic and volatile political climate. Long-standing prejudice against Japanese immigrants and their American-born children, fueled by economic jealousy and xenophobia, was now amplified by the specter of a foreign enemy who shared their ancestry.[1]

In this super-heated environment, demands for the removal of all people of Japanese descent from the West Coast grew from a racist fringe to a mainstream political position. Faced with immense public pressure and the racially charged advice of military leaders, President Franklin D. Roosevelt's administration failed to find a course of moderation. In

February 1942, the President signed Executive Order 9066.[2] This order did not name a specific group, but it authorized the military to designate vast areas of the country as zones from which "any or all persons may be excluded." This brief, bureaucratic document became the legal instrument that transformed decades of prejudice and a moment of panic into one of the most sweeping deprivations of civil liberties in American history.

3.2 : The Bureaucracy of Internment

The power of Executive Order 9066 lay not in a passionate constitutional argument, but in the cold, efficient language of modern bureaucracy. Unlike Lincoln's direct and personal defense of his actions, the order itself is remarkably sterile. It names no specific group and makes no grand claims about presidential power. Instead, it functions as an administrative delegation of authority, granting immense and vaguely defined power to the Secretary of War. This bureaucratic approach was insidious; it allowed for a massive and racially targeted deprivation of liberty to be carried out under the guise of neutral military planning. It sidestepped a direct debate about constitutional rights by framing the issue as a simple matter of military logistics, in stark contrast to the overt constitutional crisis of the Civil War.

3.3 : The Cautious Court and the Loyal Citizen

The judicial response to this new form of administrative detention came in the landmark habeas corpus case of *Ex parte Endo*.[3] The case was brought by Mitsuye Endo, an American citizen of Japanese descent who was fired from her civil service job and sent to an internment camp. Crucially, the government later conceded that she was a "loyal and law-abiding citizen." The question before the Supreme Court, therefore, was not about the initial evacuation, but whether the government had the authority to continue imprisoning a citizen whose loyalty was not in question.

In a unanimous but carefully narrow ruling, the Supreme Court ordered Endo's release. The Court, however, deliberately avoided the explosive constitutional question of the internment itself. Instead of making a broad declaration, it focused on statutory interpretation. It found that while Executive Order 9066 authorized the military to exclude people from military areas, neither the order nor any act of Congress explicitly authorized the indefinite detention of a concededly loyal citizen.[4] This act of judicial restraint was a strategic masterclass; it allowed the Court to grant freedom to an individual without directly confronting the immense power of a popular wartime president, showcasing a judiciary navigating a treacherous political landscape.

3.4 : A Legacy of Infamy

Ultimately, the Japanese-American internment represents a catastrophic failure of all three branches of the American government. The **Executive Branch**, led by President Roosevelt, succumbed to political pressure and racist counsel, ignoring its own intelligence that contradicted the need for the policy.[5] The **Legislative Branch** failed in its oversight role, instead passing legislation that ratified the executive order and added

criminal penalties to its

enforcement.[6]

And while the **Judicial Branch** provided a sliver of relief in *Ex parte Endo*, its cautious, narrow ruling was also a form of failure. The Supreme Court's decision to free one "concededly loyal" citizen while deliberately avoiding the larger constitutional question of the internment itself meant that the systemic injustice was left unchallenged at the highest level. The case of Mitsuye Endo shows that even when the writ of habeas corpus provides an individual remedy, it can be a weak and timid check against immense executive and legislative power fueled by widespread public fear. It is a sobering lesson on the fragility of liberty when the entire machinery of government and public opinion is mobilized against a single, powerless group.

Chapter 3 Summary:

- Following Pearl Harbor, a combination of war hysteria and racism led to President Roosevelt's Executive Order 9066, which authorized the internment of Japanese

Americans.

- The order was a bureaucratic delegation of power, avoiding the direct constitutional arguments seen in the Civil War.
- In *Ex parte Endo*, the Supreme Court ordered the release of a loyal citizen on narrow, statutory grounds, but deliberately avoided ruling on the constitutionality of the internment itself.
- The episode is a case study in the failure of all three branches of government to protect civil liberties during a popular war.

Notes

1. Richard Reeves, *Infamy: The Shocking Story of the Japanese American Internment in World War II* (New York: Henry Holt and Co., 2015), 33-40.
2. Exec. Order No. 9066, 7 Fed. Reg. 1407 (Feb. 19, 1942).
3. *Ex parte Endo*, 323 U.S. 283 (1944).
4. *Endo*, 323 U.S. at 302.
5. The "Munson Report," delivered to the White House in

November 1941, is a key piece of evidence for this claim.

See Reeves, *Infamy*, 70-73.

6. Pub. L. No. 77-503, 56 Stat. 173 (1942).

Chapter 4: The "War on Terror": Guantanamo Bay and the Redefinition of the Writ

4.1 : A New Paradigm of War

The terrorist attacks of September 11, 2001, were a national trauma that fundamentally reshaped the American legal and political landscape. In their aftermath, the United States embarked upon a "War on Terror"—a new kind of conflict that was not against a nation-state, but against a diffuse global network. It was a war with no clear battlefields, no uniformed enemy, and no foreseeable end. In response to this unprecedented challenge, the U.S. Congress, with near unanimity, passed the **Authorization for Use of Military Force (AUMF)** just days after the attacks.[1] This brief document was a vast and open-ended grant of power, authorizing the President to use "all necessary and appropriate force" against those responsible. This "blank check" became the foundational legal pillar upon which the next two decades of detention, surveillance, and military action would be built.

4.2 : The Law of the Camp

Acting on the broad authority of the AUMF, the executive branch established a detention facility at the U.S. Naval Base at Guantanamo Bay, Cuba. This location was deliberately chosen. The administration's legal theory was that because the base was outside of the sovereign territory of the United States, the detainees held there were beyond the reach of the U.S. Constitution and, most importantly, had no right to petition federal courts for a writ of habeas corpus.[2] It was an attempt to create a legal "black hole," a space where individuals could be detained indefinitely without judicial oversight.

After early Supreme Court decisions began to challenge this theory, the legislative branch intervened to reinforce the executive's position. In the **Detainee Treatment Act (DTA)** of 2005 and the **Military Commissions Act (MCA)** of 2006, Congress built a legislative wall around the camp.[3] In a move reminiscent of *Ex parte McCardle*, these acts explicitly stripped federal courts of their jurisdiction to hear habeas petitions from Guantanamo detainees. In place of the writ, Congress created a system of military-run tribunals (CSRTs) to determine the status of detainees. This was a clear, coordinated effort by the political branches to create a separate and distinct legal system for the "War on Terror," one in which the judiciary's traditional role as the guardian of the writ was intentionally and systematically removed.

4.3 : The Constitutional Showdown

The legal and political efforts to insulate Guantanamo Bay from judicial review culminated in the landmark 2008 Supreme Court case, **Boumediene v. Bush**.[4] The case was a direct constitutional showdown, pitting the detainees' right to the writ against the combined will of the President and Congress, who had acted decisively to strip the courts of jurisdiction. The central question was profound: Could the political branches of the U.S. government create a territory under their complete control where the Constitution's most fundamental check on executive power did not apply?

In a monumental 5-4 decision, the Court answered with a qualified "no." Writing for the majority, Justice Anthony Kennedy made two critical rulings. First, the Court found that because the U.S. exercised "de facto sovereignty" and effective control over the Guantanamo Bay base— meaning it functioned as U.S. territory in all but name—the constitutional privilege of habeas corpus extended to the detainees held there.[5] Second, the Court held that the alternative review process created by Congress—the CSRTs— was an inadequate and unconstitutional substitute for a meaningful habeas hearing.[6] Therefore, the section of the Military Commissions Act that stripped the courts of jurisdiction was an unconstitutional suspension of the writ.

The ruling was a powerful reassertion of judicial authority, a modern echo of *Bollman*'s claim that the judiciary is the ultimate guardian of the writ. However, the fiery dissent from justices like Antonin Scalia, who accused the majority of unprecedented judicial overreach in wartime, highlighted the deep and enduring nature of this constitutional conflict.[7]

4.4 : An Unsettled State

The Supreme Court's decision in *Boumediene v. Bush* was a landmark victory for the writ of habeas corpus and a powerful assertion of judicial power. However, it was not a final resolution. The razor-thin 5-4 majority revealed a Court, and a nation, deeply divided on the fundamental balance between national security and individual liberty. The ruling did not close the Guantanamo Bay detention camp, nor did it end the political and legal battles over the detainees. It simply shifted the conflict from the question of if the courts had jurisdiction to the complex and contentious question of what process the detainees were due.

The legacy of the War on Terror's legal battles is, therefore, an unsettled one. The *Boumediene* decision reaffirmed the judiciary's role as a critical check on the political branches, proving that the great writ could not be easily legislated away. Yet, the fierce dissent and the ongoing political controversies demonstrate that the foundational tension we have traced throughout this book—the struggle between state power and individual liberty in a time of crisis—is not a problem that can be definitively "solved." It is a permanent and defining feature of the American constitutional system, with the state of the great writ remaining as contested and vital as ever.

Chapter 4 Summary:

- Following the 9/11 attacks, Congress granted the President vast power through the 2001 AUMF.
- The Guantanamo Bay detention camp was established, with the executive and legislative branches attempting to place it outside the reach of U.S. courts via the DTA and MCA.
- In *Boumediene v. Bush*, the Supreme Court ruled 5-4 that the writ of habeas corpus does extend to Guantanamo and that Congress's attempt to strip jurisdiction was an unconstitutional suspension of the writ.
- The ruling was a major assertion of judicial power but did not end the legal and political debates, highlighting that the core constitutional tension remains unresolved.

Notes

1. Authorization for Use of Military Force, Pub. L. No. 107-40, 115 Stat. 224 (2001).

2. John Yoo, "The President's Constitutional Authority to Conduct Military Operations Against Terrorist Organizations and the Nations that Harbor Them," Office of Legal Counsel Memorandum, September 25, 2001.

3. Detainee Treatment Act of 2005, Pub. L. No. 109-148, 119 Stat. 2739;

4. Military Commissions Act of 2006, Pub. L. No. 109-366, 120 Stat. 2600.

5. *Boumediene v. Bush*, 553 U.S. 723 (2008).

6. *Boumediene*, 553 U.S. at 764.

7. *Boumediene*, 553 U.S. at 792.

8. *Boumediene*, 553 U.S. at 827 (Scalia, J., dissenting).

Chapter 5: The Unfinished Argument

5.1 : The Enduring Tension

As this history has shown, the story of the writ of habeas corpus in the United States is not one of a steady, triumphant march of liberty. It is the story of an enduring, and often fierce, constitutional tension. The foundational conflict established in the 19th century—between the judiciary's role as the writ's guardian, as asserted in *Bollman*, and the political branches' claims of crisis-driven necessity, as seen in *McCardle*—has never been permanently resolved. It has instead been re-litigated and re-fought in every major era of the nation's history. This tension was stretched to its breaking point by President Lincoln's unilateral actions during the Civil War, cautiously sidestepped by the Supreme Court amid the racist hysteria of World War II, and ultimately brought to a dramatic head in the 21st-century showdown over Guantanamo Bay.

5.2 : The State of the Writ Today

In the present day, the legacy of the battles fought in *Boumediene* is a complex one. While the Supreme Court's decision was a landmark legal victory for the rule of law, its practical impact has been slow and contested. The political branches have been reluctant to create a clear and final resolution for the remaining detainees, leaving many in an indefinite legal limbo. This demonstrates that a judicial victory for the writ does not always translate into immediate or comprehensive political action.

Beyond Guantanamo, the great writ continues to be a central battleground in modern American law, particularly in the context of immigration detention. Legal challenges are constantly being waged over whether the writ can be used to contest prolonged detention for non-citizens awaiting asylum hearings or deportation. Furthermore, the continued existence of the open-ended 2001 Authorization for Use of Military Force means that the legal framework that enabled the War on Terror's detention policies remains in place. The fundamental questions about the balance of power in a state of perpetual emergency are not historical; they are the pressing legal questions of our time.

5.3 : The Future of the Great Writ

The history we have traced proves that the great writ is both resilient and fragile. Its core principle—that no person shall be held without a lawful reason—has survived civil war, world wars, and the dawn of global terrorism. Yet, its power has always been contingent on the political climate and, most importantly, on the courage of an independent judiciary to uphold it against the claims of necessity.

The future will undoubtedly bring new crises that will test the writ in unforeseen ways. The challenges may no longer be rebellious armies or foreign powers, but the silent encroachments of mass surveillance, the complexities of cyber warfare where combatants are invisible, or the domestic turmoil wrought by pandemics and extreme political polarization. Each new crisis will present the same timeless question in a new form: will the rule of law bend to the will of power? The story of habeas corpus teaches us that the writ is not a self-enforcing shield. It is a tool, and its effectiveness depends entirely on the willingness of citizens to demand it and judges to grant it. The unfinished argument, therefore, is not one that can be settled by a single book or a single court case. It is the permanent, ongoing work of the nation itself. To protect the great writ is to protect the essence of a free society, and that solemn responsibility rests not only with the courts, but with every citizen.

Glossary

AUMF (Authorization for Use of Military Force): The 2001 act passed by Congress just after the September 11th attacks, which granted the President broad and open-ended authority to use military force against those responsible. It became the primary legal justification for the War on Terror.

CSRT (Combatant Status Review Tribunal): A type of military-run hearing created by the U.S. government during the War on Terror to determine if a detainee at Guantanamo Bay was properly classified as an "enemy combatant." The Supreme Court later found this process to be an inadequate substitute for a habeas corpus hearing.

De Facto Sovereignty: A situation where a country exercises the practical power and control of a government over a territory, even if it doesn't have official legal ownership or "sovereignty" over it. This was the Supreme Court's key argument for extending constitutional protections to Guantanamo Bay in *Boumediene v. Bush*.

DTA (Detainee Treatment Act): A 2005 act of Congress that, among other things, attempted to strip federal courts of jurisdiction over habeas corpus petitions from Guantanamo detainees.

Due Process: A fundamental constitutional guarantee that all legal proceedings will be fair and that one will be given notice of the proceedings and an opportunity to be heard before the government can take away life, liberty, or property.

Enemy Combatant: A term used, particularly during the War on Terror, to describe a person considered to be engaged in hostilities against the United States but who is not part of a formal state army. Their legal status and rights have been a subject of major debate.

Executive Order: A directive issued by the President of the United States that manages operations of the federal government. It has the force of law. Executive Order 9066 was the directive that authorized the Japanese-American internment.

Habeas Corpus: (Latin for "you shall have the body.") The legal procedure, often called "the great writ," that allows a prisoner to challenge the legality of their detention before a court. It is a fundamental check on the power of the executive branch to imprison individuals without a lawful reason.

Jurisdiction: The official power of a court to make legal decisions and judgments in a particular case or geographic area. An act of "jurisdiction-stripping" is when Congress passes a law to remove a court's authority to hear a specific type of case.

MCA (Military Commissions Act): A 2006 act of Congress that further tried to strip court jurisdiction over detainee cases and authorized the use of military commissions to try detainees for war crimes.

Military Tribunal / Military Commission: A type of court run by the military, rather than the civilian court system. Their use to try civilians or non-citizen detainees has been a source of major constitutional conflict throughout U.S. history.

Statute: A formal written law passed by a legislative body like Congress.

Statutory Interpretation: The process by which courts interpret and apply legislation. Sometimes, a court will rule on a narrow statutory basis (what a specific law allows) to avoid making a broader ruling on the constitutionality of that law.

Suspension Clause: The clause in the U.S. Constitution (Article I, Section 9) that protects the privilege of the writ of habeas corpus, stating that it "shall not be suspended, unless when in Cases of Rebellion or Invasion the public Safety may require it."

Writ: A formal written order issued by a court.

Bibliography

Cases

- *Boumediene v. Bush*, 553 U.S. 723 (2008).
- *Ex parte Bollman*, 8 U.S. 75 (1807).
- *Ex parte Endo*, 323 U.S. 283 (1944).
- *Ex parte McCardle*, 74 U.S. 506 (1869).
- *Ex parte Milligan*, 71 U.S. 2 (1866).

Statutes and Executive Orders

- Authorization for Use of Military Force. Pub. L. No. 107-40, 115 Stat. 224. Enacted September 18, 2001.
- Detainee Treatment Act of 2005. Pub. L. No. 109-148, 119

- Stat. 2739. Enacted December 30, 2005.
- Executive Order 9066, "Authorizing the Secretary of War to Prescribe Certain Areas as Military Areas." 7 Fed. Reg. 1407 (February 19, 1942).
- Magna Carta (1215).
- Military Commissions Act of 2006. Pub. L. No. 109-366, 120 Stat. 2600. Enacted October 17, 2006.
- U.S. Constitution.

Books and Articles

- Halliday, Paul D. *Habeas Corpus: From England to Empire*. Cambridge, MA: Belknap Press, 2010.
- Lincoln, Abraham. "Message to Congress in Special Session." Washington, D.C., July 4, 1861.
- Neely Jr., Mark E. *The Fate of Liberty: Abraham Lincoln and Civil Liberties*. New York: Oxford University Press, 1991.
- Reeves, Richard. *Infamy: The Shocking Story of the Japanese American Internment in World War II*. New York: Henry Holt and Co., 2015.
- Yoo, John. "The President's Constitutional Authority to

Conduct Military Operations Against Terrorist Organizations and the Nations that Harbor Them." Office of Legal Counsel Memorandum, September 25, 2001.

About The Author

Kerry Khan has spent years navigating the complex and often fraught relationship between state power and individual freedom. Drawing on a unique synthesis of legal training from The Catholic University of America and advanced strategic studies at the National Defense University, he has dedicated himself to one of the most fundamental principles of law: the writ of habeas corpus.

The Great Writ: A Nation's Struggle with Liberty and Power is the product of that singular focus—an unflinching and comprehensive analysis forged from centuries of **case law, executive orders, and congressional acts.**

www.ingramcontent.com/pod-product-compliance
Lightning Source LLC
Chambersburg PA
CBHW050919160426
43194CB00011B/2474